Rodeo Clowns

Paul Kupperberg

rosen central™

The Rosen Publishing Group, Inc., New York

Published in 2006 by The Rosen Publishing Group, Inc.
29 East 21st Street, New York, NY 10010

First Edition

Library of Congress Cataloging-in-Publication Data

Kupperberg, Paul.
Rodeo clowns/by Paul Kupperberg.
        p. cm.—(The world of rodeo)
Includes bibliographical references and index.
ISBN 1-4042-0546-2 (library binding)
1. Rodeo clowns—United States—History—Juvenile literature. 2. Rodeos—United
States—History—Juvenile literature. I. Title. II. Series.
GV1834.5.K86 2005
791.8'4—dc22

                                                                      2005014917

Manufactured in Malaysia

On the cover: A rodeo clown distracts an angry bull from trampling a fallen rider at a high school competition in Colorado.

Contents

Before anyone ever heard of extreme sports or the X Games, cowboys were riding bucking broncs and wild bulls and roping and wrestling savage steers in rodeos. What could be more extreme than sitting bareback atop a bucking 2,000-pound (907 kilogram) bull, holding on to nothing more than a thin leather strap? What sport could be more dangerous than one that involves bringing down a 700-pound (318 kg) raging steer bare-handed?

The answer can be found in the same rodeo arenas where skilled cowboys exercise amazing athletic abilities, and it might surprise you. Although they may seem like ridiculous figures in garish makeup and outlandish costumes, rodeo clowns have some of the most dangerous jobs in one of the world's most dangerous sports. The rodeo clown is much more than a character to be laughed at. He is the royal jester of the rodeo arena who is also responsible for protecting cowboys from the hooves and horns of bulls.

The rodeo clown's high jinks may look easy, but under the silly outfits and makeup he is a trained athlete entrusted with a life-and-death mission every day he is in the arena. The rodeo clown's job is no joking matter.

Two rodeo clowns work as a team to get an excited bull's attention. This diversion will allow the rider on the far right to crawl to safety. Rodeo clowns usually wear loose clothing with bright colors or patterns. Although this clothing gives rodeo clowns an amusing appearance, it is also designed to tear away if snagged by a bull's horns.

FROM ROUNDUP TO SHOW BUSINESS

CHAPTER 1

Though no one can truly say when and where the first organized rodeo was held, we know that they began as early as the seventeenth century in Mexico (then known as New Spain). Spanish settlers arrived in what is now known as the Americas two decades before the Pilgrims landed at Plymouth Rock. To them, the earliest *rodear* were simple cattle roundups, where the grazing cattle were rounded up and brought to one central market. After long, lonely months on the trails, *vaqueros* (from the Spanish words for "cow" and "man") used these occasions to hold impromptu competitions. They would show off their skills at roping, riding, and breaking wild broncos. "There were few things [the vaqueros] couldn't do from a saddle," Kendall Nelson, a photographer who documents the life of today's working cowboys, told a reporter for Nationalgeographic.com.

These gatherings spread north into what was to become the Texas territory of the United States, and then across the American West. "All of the skills, traditions, and ways of working with cattle are very much rooted in the Mexican vaquero," Nelson said. "If you are a cowboy in the U.S. today, you have developed what you know from the vaquero."

Part of what these cowboys learned was the way of the rodear. The first documented organized rodeo is believed to have been held on July 4, 1864, in Prescott, Arizona. Exactly five years later, another one was held in Deer Trail,

A cowboy rides a bucking bronco in this 1922 photograph. Also known as mustangs or cayuses, broncos are wild horses that reside in western North America. Bronc riding is one of the oldest rodeo competitions, and participants can either ride in the saddle or bareback divisions. Saddle bronc riding is considered by many to be the "classic" rodeo event.

Colorado. There, an Englishman named Emilnie Gardenshire earned the title Champion Bronco Buster of the Plains and the prize of a new suit of clothes for a fifteen-minute ride on a horse named Montana Blizzard. In modern rodeos, riders must stay on a bronc for a mere eight seconds, but the original cowboys simply rode until they or their horses gave up.

The Western entertainer Buffalo Bill Cody, originator of the Wild West show, began using the term "rodeo" for his shows, which included roping, riding, bronc breaking, and bull riding. Once the humble rodeo went from a competition to a popular form of entertainment, it needed more than cowboys to keep the show moving. It was here that the rodeo clown was born.

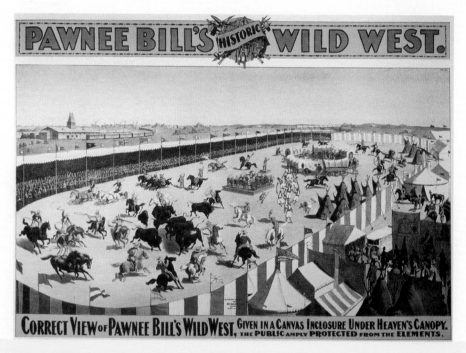

A poster from 1894 advertises Pawnee Bill's Wild West show. Pawnee Bill's real name was Gordon William Lillie. He received his nickname from a Native American tribe in Oklahoma. Pawnee Bill worked for Buffalo Bill's Wild West show for five years before starting his own in 1888. The show ran for twenty years before it finally merged with Buffalo Bill's show.

SEND IN THE CLOWNS

As rodeos began charging admission to spectators, the organizers needed to keep the customers entertained and happy during the delays between events. The first rodeo clowns were cowboys who could amuse the audience with their antics, such as Tin Horn Hank Keenan. Tin Horn Hank began his career in rodeos in 1912 as a cowboy. Soon after, he found he possessed a talent for getting laughs from an audience and became one of the earliest known clowns on the rodeo circuit. His son, Carl, born and raised on the rodeo circuit, learned how to trick ride and rope. Carl eventually joined his father's act as Little Tin Horn.

Charley Schultz of Clayton, New Mexico, discovered his ability to make people laugh when he donned an old circus clown costume to entertain neighbors at a Fourth of July picnic in 1914. Inspired by the laughter, he spent the rest of his life as a rodeo clown.

Clowns quickly caught on and began appearing in rodeos across the West. In the 1915 rodeo season, the Miller Brothers and Arlington 101 Ranch Real Wild West show introduced three clowns, Bill Caress, Billy Lorette, and Joe Lewis.

To earn a steady income, these clowns would also appear in Wild West shows. Wild West shows featured reenactments of famous cowboy-and-Indian battles and exhibitions of cowboy skills rather than the competitions common to rodeos. It would be several decades before the rodeo would supplant the Wild West show as the more popular form of entertainment.

One of the earliest clowns was Dan Dix, whose antics at the Cheyenne

The Frontier Days rodeo in Cheyenne, Wyoming, has been delighting audiences for nearly 110 years. It was started in 1897 as a way to bring new visitors to the isolated region, and is considered to be the biggest outdoor rodeo in the world. It also features a Native American village, an Old West museum, and antique horse-drawn carriages.

(Wyoming) Frontier Days were typical of these early entertainers. As described by Robert D. Hanesworth in his book, *Daddy of 'Em All: The Story of Cheyenne Frontier Days*, Dix would attempt "to get his mule to move by pulling and jerking on a rope fastened to the halter. In response, the mule laid down. Dan then talked nicely to him and everything was rosy again."

The Brahman Bull

In his book *Rodeo: Back of the Chutes*, Gene Lamb writes, "The Brahma bull can claim credit for a lot of employment in rodeo, because without him there would be no need for the clowns. Up until the 1920s bull riding was not a predominant event in rodeo. The 'bulls' might be real bulls, they might be range cows, they might be good-sized steers; in fact, they might be anything that could be remotely considered a 'bull.'"

No one knows who introduced Brahman bulls to the rodeo. Many people think that a man named Verne Elliot, who brought Brahmans to a Fort Worth, Texas, rodeo in the 1920s, is responsible. The bulls were very popular, and it wasn't long until they were featured at virtually every major rodeo in the world.

Since riders could be killed by out of control bulls, the rodeo clown's job became even more important.

While perhaps not the most sophisticated of acts, in the days before television, radio, and films, these simple entertainments were enough to keep the crowd enthralled. Over time, the acts became more complex, with early stars Homer Holcomb and Red Sublett and his trained mule Spark Plug combining clown antics with increasingly dangerous stunts.

LAUGHTER AND DANGER

For the first decade or so of rodeo clowning, the baggy-pants-wearing, painted-face clown was concerned largely with getting laughs. This changed in the late 1920s, when the ferocious Brahman bull was introduced into the bull-riding event.

In a 1954 article in the rodeo trade publication *Hoofs & Horns*, editor Ethel A. Hopkins called them "the meanest animal on Earth. It is . . . nearly a ton of

A rodeo clown stares down a Brahman bull, one of the most ferocious animals on the planet. Although they amuse the audience, the rodeo clown's job is an extremely dangerous one. Rodeo clowns risk their lives to keep cowboys safe in the arena, and many have been injured and even killed by Brahman bulls.

concentrated dynamite. An animal with the strength of Samson, cunning of a fox, sight of an eagle, speed of an antelope, and the vile heart of a Black Widow spider" (as quoted in *Fearless Funnymen: The History of the Rodeo Clown* by Gail Hughbanks Woerner).

Brahman bulls will charge at the rider after he's been thrown or jumps off at the end of his qualifying ride. These one-ton behemoths will attack anything that gets in their path. To save the bull riders from serious injury, the rodeo "bullfighter" was born. These bullfighters differ from the traditional Spanish bullfighters, or matadors, whose objective is to kill the bull. The rodeo bullfighter's job is to distract the bull long enough to allow a downed rider to get to safety. At the rodeo, the bull lives to be ridden another day.

Rodeo Clowns

Homer Holcomb, a clown working for Verne Elliott at the time, is believed to have been the first of this courageous breed of clown. He would race out into the arena after the rider had been thrown or jumped, making himself the bull's target while riders on horseback corralled the irate beast out the exit gate. "Often the clown's skill makes the difference in whether the cowboy goes to the next rodeo, hospital or a morgue," wrote Sam Savitt in his book, *Rodeo: Cowboys, Bulls, and Broncos.*

Bullfighters are often teamed with a barrelman, a specialty role originated by a clown named Jasbo Fulkerson. The barrelman remains, literally, in a barrel in the arena during the cowboy's ride. He emerges only to distract the bull if needed, then retreats back into the barrel for protection from the charging animal.

F. J. "Scooter" Culbertson, a professional rodeo clown, bullfighter, and barrelman, told the Web site Essortment.com, "Getting hit by a bull is like getting hit by a car going twenty miles [thirty-two kilometers] an hour. It's not if you are going to get hurt. It's when and how bad."

And yet it is a job rodeo clowns and bullfighters do on a regular basis, all the while keeping the audience laughing.

TOP CLOWNS

CHAPTER 2

There's hardly a stunt rodeo clowns won't attempt or a risk they won't take to do their jobs. Over the years, these Wild West jesters have pulled off stunts that would make even professional Hollywood stuntmen back away in doubt. Imagine riding a bucking horse or wild steer; now imagine doing the same thing, only riding backward or sitting in a washtub bolted to a saddle. Considering the difficulty of what they do, only the most skilled cowboys can hope to make it as a clown.

From the very beginning, clowns devised stunts that were more and more hazardous in their quest to keep the audience amused and to top not only themselves but their fellow clowns. Many of the routines and stunts they've created over the years have become classics, and are performed in rodeos across the United States and Canada to this very day.

RED SUBLETT, RODEO'S FIRST FAMOUS CLOWN

Born in 1894 in Texas and raised in Oklahoma, John Dixon "Red" Sublett spent his life around cowboys, horses, and cattle. He worked for a time with Wild West shows and then bummed around the Texas panhandle as a cowboy and rider. Red wanted an opportunity to travel and see the country, so he joined up again with a Wild West show.

Red Sublett slides off a sitting mule in this postcard *(above)*. Sublett's favorite mule was named Spark Plug. He taught Spark Plug to imitate trained horses in the middle of their performances, an act that earned them many laughs. Red Sublett poses with fellow cowboy Tommie Douglas in this photograph *(right)*. Sublett is standing on the right.

Thanks to his talent as a versatile stock rider, Red quickly became a featured performer in the show. He claimed he could ride anything that a saddle, rigging, or rope could be attached to, and that claim was constantly put to the test. He rode bucking horses, steers, bulls, and even cows, as well as mules, buffalo, and zebras. Once, he even rode an ostrich.

After serving in the army during World War I, Red returned to the rodeo circuit and grew famous for his unorthodox style, which included coming out of the chute riding a bull or bronc backward. It was only natural for Red to make the move from his laugh-getting antics as a cowboy to the full-time job of rodeo clown. Red Sublett was rodeo's number-one clown for many years, working every big show in North America, as well as traveling overseas to perform in London, England; Mexico City, Mexico; Brussels, Belgium; and Dublin, Ireland. He even went to Hollywood to appear in movies.

TIN HORN HANK KEENAN, CHAMPION CLOWN

Born around 1895, Hank Keenan got his start as a teenager in 1912 with Wild West shows such as the 101 Ranch Real Wild West Show. He rode steers and broncs with or without a saddle, wrestled steers, and rode in wild-horse races.

Tin Horn Hank didn't start clowning full-time until 1929. According to a 1984 article in the *Western Horseman*, "Because he was such an excellent bronc rider, he made difficult acts look easy. He often strapped a tin tub to a bronc, got inside and then rode the horse out of a chute. Records indicate he rode some of the top mounts of the era . . . Once, at McLaughlin County Fair [in Nebraska] the committee offered $500 to anybody who could make an eight-jump ride on the mighty Tipperary [that is, to stay on a famously difficult bronc while the horse bucked at least eight times]. Not knowing quite what to expect, Hank mounted up—and won the money."

In the same article, Hank's son Carl recalled that a typical day of clowning for his father would include "Riding a couple of steers backwards while holding a suitcase and firing a pistol; riding a couple of broncs holding a suitcase and firing a blazing .45, stepping off and turning cartwheels; clowning on [his mule] Steembote; clowning

Tin Horn Hank Keenan was an accomplished trick rider. In this undated photograph, he makes riding a wild horse look easy. He holds a suitcase while a crowd of cowboys admires his showmanship.

up some kind of quick ambulance ride [in the ambulance that stood at the ready in the event of accidents]; driving a steer or bull attached to a Roman chariot; trick riding on a mule; shooting act with a pig; a bullwhip act; funnying up the wild cow milking and wild horse race; and fighting bulls when crossbred Brahmas began to replace domestic steers."

HOMER HOLCOMB, BULLFIGHTER

Homer Holcomb began clowning in 1919 in Spokane, Washington, and grew to fame as the sport's first bullfighter. Though a world relay riding champion and all-around cowboy, he turned to clowning and earned a reputation for fearlessness. Holcomb's lack of fear allowed him to become the first man to enter the arena as a human target for a riled up Brahman bull.

An article in a 1941 issue of *Hoofs & Horns* about Holcomb said, "At least 3,000 times a year, Homer rushes in to protect bull riders after they have jumped or been thrown off Brahma bulls. At least 3,000 times a year Homer waves his red cape in the face of a maddened, pawing, snorting Brahman; taunts him to give chase; escapes by clever footwork then scurries to the nearest barrier bare seconds before slashing horns lash out, capable of tearing him to shreds."

JASBO FULKERSON, RODEO'S BARRELMAN

Equally fearless was Jasbo Fulkerson, rodeo's first barrelman. He gave up bareback and bull riding in 1927 to start clowning. As he told the authors of *Jasbo*, people

Jasbo Fulkerson shows why he was a crowd favorite in this photograph from a 1937 rodeo. He is riding a homemade chariot attached to a burly Brahman. Fulkerson was a star rodeo clown, and was one of the first people to be inducted into the Pro Rodeo Hall of Fame when it opened in 1979.

took rodeos too seriously, with "everybody all scrunched down in their seats pullin' on their hats like it was life and death, so I figured I'd make them laugh." And make them laugh he did, for twenty-five successful years. Willard Porter, a reporter for the *Daily Oklahoman*, called Fulkerson "naturally funny . . . He was cowboy enough to parody each event, and he had both a sense of the dramatic and ridiculous. This, of course, helped him when he roped a steer on his mule and the mule was jerked down."

Fulkerson brought not only laughs but innovation to the rodeo arena. His most famous contribution was an invention born out of necessity. "Here his short stature was responsible for his famous trademark—the big red barrel," recalled cowboy Foghorn Clancy in his autobiography, *My Fifty Years in the Rodeo*. "While

Women Performers

A photo of Tad Lucas from the 1930s.

Rodeo clowning has never really been a popular career choice for women. Still, there have been a handful of female clowns who have left their mark on the field:

- **Tad Lucas**, a female bronc rider and trick rider, was asked to clown in Verne Elliott's show after the death of Jasbo Fulkerson in 1949. Filling in for Fulkerson and working with clowns John Lindsey and George Mills for thirteen shows, she was popular enough that she would occasionally work shows as a clown in addition to her regular appearances as a trick rider.

- **Juanita Gray** was a trick rider who had long had the urge to try her hand at clowning before a producer let her in the arena as a bullfighter.

- **Dixie Mosley** began her rodeo career as a trick rider on a Shetland pony at the age of five. She started clowning when she was eleven years old, and was the only official clown of the Girl's Rodeo Association.

- **Bonnie Eloise Williams** started in rodeo as a trick rider. In 1979, in order to land a job with a booker who was trying to decide between her and a barrelman, Williams told him she would do both jobs if he hired her.

Foghorn Clancy, whose real name was Frederick Melton Clancy, was a popular rodeo announcer for more than forty years. He supposedly received his nickname while selling newspapers during the Spanish-American War. In addition to being an announcer, Clancy was also a published author. He wrote many articles about the rodeo for Western-themed magazines, as well as an autobiography about his long career.

he could sidestep the rushes of the bull for a long time, his stubby legs handicapped him in a long run to the arena wall—a race he was bound to lose." This became his "sanctuary in the center of the arena." Thus, a barrel reinforced with old automobile tires made Jasbo Fulkerson a rodeo legend.

MONKEYS, MULES, MAGIC, AND BUCKING CARS

Like any good performers in show business, rodeo clowns often have specialty acts that make them stand out.

Red Sublett goes for a joyride on a bucking Ford in this photograph. The legendary rodeo clown was performing at the Magruder Brothers Ski-Hi Stampede in Monte Vista, Colorado. Sublett was the highest-paid clown of his time. If rodeo promoters wanted the best, they asked for Red Sublett.

Bill Harbison, for instance, took the feared Brahman bull and made it a partner in his act. As Brahma Bill and his trained steer Buster, they were immensely popular on the rodeo circuit. According to a January 1938 article in *Hoofs & Horns*, "Buster, transformed from one of the meanest Brahmas in any man's string of rodeo stock, has responded to Bill's skill … in a way that has to be seen to be believed. Buster not only does as he is told, but Buster really loves the show, and is as much the clown as Bill is, and Bill is a 'natural'" (as quoted in *Fearless Funnymen: The History of the Rodeo Clown*).

Animals of all sorts were natural partners for the rodeo clown. John Lindsey worked with a trained miniature Hereford bull, Iron Ore, and Diamond D. Dewey with a 1,000-pound (454 kg) trained buffalo. Andy Womack had a trained chimp named Jocko, and Wilbur Plaugher's act included a dog that herded ducks. Wes Curtis had a flock of trained chickens.

Horses were, of course, common sidekicks for the clowns, but according to an article in the *Ketch Pen*, the official publication of the Rodeo Historical Society, "Every good clown must have a mule." The O'Neill Brothers, clowns who worked with the lady mule Skimmilk, told *Hoofs & Horns* in 1939, "Mules are smarter than horses. But that does not mean that mules are easier to train or to work with … On the contrary, a horse will not cheat very much as you put him through his tricks because he is not smart enough. But a mule, though he learns his tricks much more readily, is so smart that he learns to cheat and

Gene and Bobby Clark engage in a bit of monkey business for the camera in this 1966 photograph. The brothers became very popular for their hilarious antics, and were also very respected for their bullfighting abilities. Besides being rodeo clowns, both brothers also competed in the calf-roping events. The Clark brothers were inducted into the Pro Rodeo Hall of Fame in 1997.

you have to watch them all the time" (as quoted in *Fearless Funnymen: The History of the Rodeo Clown*).

Cheats or not, many of the clown stars of rodeo worked with mules. Some became almost as famous as their human sidekicks, from Red Sublett's Spark Plug and Hoyt Hefner's Martha Raye to Jimmy Nesbitt's Billy Sunday, Jasbo Fulkerson's Eko, and Charley Shultz's Judy.

Tim Lepard is a world champion rodeo clown who is more famous for working with monkeys than with bulls. Lepard is pictured here with Suzie, a capuchin monkey, and King, a Border collie. They are members of his comedy troupe. Lepard trains capuchin monkeys to herd sheep while riding saddleback on border collies.

Bobby and Gene Clark were brothers who brought a little magic into their act. In Kannon Kapers, Bobby would disappear in a puff of smoke after Gene shot him with a cannon, only to appear elsewhere in the arena. Husband and wife clowns Clark and Arlene Shultz became famous for their comedy car act, utilizing what was to become a standard rodeo prop, the bucking car. This is a tricked-out car that bounces and bucks like a bronc.

There was no limit to how far these clowns would go in pursuit of a laugh, whether diving into a barrel to escape a charging bull, strapping washtubs and rocking chairs to the backs of bucking stock, riding two men to a bronc, or hitching a two-wheel chariot to a Brahman bull. Modern-day clowns such as Bert Davis, Nick Jensen, Rob Smets, and Canada's Dennis Halstead continue the traditions begun almost a century ago, giving their all for the safety of the riders and the enjoyment of the audience.

A DANGEROUS PROFESSION

CHAPTER 3

Until the Rodeo Association of America, consisting of the producers and organizers of rodeos, was formed in 1929, rodeo was a fairly rough-and-tumble sport. It lacked standardized events and rules for competition, timing, judging, arena conditions, and refereeing. The performers themselves did not organize for better pay and improved conditions until 1936, forming the Cowboy Turtle Association (CTA), which included the signatures of rodeo clowns Hoyt Hefner and Jimmy Nesbitt on its founding document.

Eventually, the CTA merged with a variety of regional rodeo associations that formed in its wake, becoming the Rodeo Cowboy Association. Finally, in 1975, it became the Professional Rodeo Cowboys Association (PRCA).

TROPHIES AND RECOGNITION

While rodeo cowboys compete for numerous awards and championship titles at the National Finals Rodeo and other competitions, clowns, bullfighters, and barrelmen have few such contests that offer them the opportunity to be crowned the best in their field. One of the only such competitions was the Wrangler Bullfight Tour, begun in 1980 and sponsored by the manufacturers of blue jeans and Western wear. The finals, held every December during the National Finals in Las Vegas, brought the top six bullfighters in the country together to compete for prize money and the championship belt buckle.

These rodeo clowns are dressed up and ready to perform at the 2004 National Finals Rodeo. Standing from left to right are Flint Rasmussen, Troy Lerwill, Seth Gorham, and Darrell Difenbach. They are waiting for the start of the bull-riding competition. The National Finals Rodeo, an important event for rodeo performers, was first held in Dallas, Texas, in 1959.

In these events, bullfighters had to spend a minimum of forty seconds in the arena with the bull, with another thirty seconds being optional. Points were awarded for how well the bullfighter could control the action and the amount of risk he was willing to take, his objective being to stay as close to the bull as he could throughout the fight. The more aggressive the bull, the higher the points awarded the successful bullfighter. The bulls, like the bullfighters, competed for years and were able to learn and improve with experience. Wrangler ended its sponsorship of the Bullfight Tour in 1999, although it remains a supporter of the National Finals. In recent years, the Professional Bull Riders (PBR) World Bullfighting Championship has taken its place as the top bullfighting competition.

Rob Smets is seen here going airborne at the 1999 National Finals Rodeo. One of America's greatest professional rodeo clowns, Smets has faced down raging bulls for more than two decades. Although he has sustained a number of very serious injuries, Smets never considered leaving the sport.

Rob "Kamikaze" Smets won the Wrangler Bullfights five times. Smets started out roping and bull riding in high school rodeos in the 1970s, but he soon discovered that he would rather be chased by the bulls than get on their backs. Despite numerous injuries—including twice breaking his neck in the arena—he has remained an active bullfighter. In 2000, the best bull riders in the world selected him to be the bullfighter for both the Professional Bullfighter Rodeo Bud Light Cup World Championships and the National Finals Rodeo. Four-time world champion bull rider Tuff Hedeman was quoted on Robsmets.com as saying, "The guys select the bullfighters, and that's the way it should be because their lives are on the line. The fact that they vote for Rob means he's still the guy they want out there (because) . . . when you're in a jam you know he's going to be right there in the middle of it. He's always jumping in there. You aren't going to meet a tougher guy." That toughness earned Smets, in addition to his Wrangler wins, five world champion bullfighter titles, six National Finals Rodeo bullfighter championships, and numerous other awards.

The Coors Brewing Company is another major sponsor of rodeo events, including their annual Coors "Man in the Can" program. The program recognizes each season's most successful PRCA barrelman, based on a competition, with cash prizes.

Like the riding and roping cowboys, clowns are eligible for induction into the PRCA Hall of Fame, the Texas Rodeo Cowboy Hall of Fame, the National Cowboy and Western Heritage Museum Hall of Fame, and other organizations.

The member cowboys of the PRCA, who are protected by these clowns, bullfighters, and barrelmen throughout the year, vote for the PRCA Clown of the Year. This is perhaps the highest honor a working clown can receive. PRCA Clown of the Year for 1989, 1990, 1991, 1993, and 1997, Butch Lehmkuhler, said in a 1990 issue of *ProRodeo Sports News*, "Receiving the awards that I received is one of the most humbling experiences that I've ever been through. So many people that I've worked with over the years took the time to stop and recognize me. It's moving."

Rodeo clowns sometimes hide in barrels to protect themselves from a charging bull. The barrel serves the same purpose as a turtle's shell: it is meant to withstand a serious attack, such as the one seen here. Jasbo Fulkerson was the first rodeo clown to use a barrel.

PROFESSIONAL ATHLETES

In recent years, ESPN has been televising rodeos and corporate sponsors have begun putting money into the sport. In this increasingly professional environment, the emphasis has shifted from the clown as simple entertainer to the more important role of bullfighter. While there are those who would like to see more of the classic routines of the funnymen of the arena, it is perhaps understandable that their role has changed.

According to an article on Salary.com, "It may look like fun and games to the people in the stands, but this is serious business, and not just any clown can do it. Between rides [their] job is to keep the crowd amused by bantering with the announcers and performing comedic skits that can include props, explosions,

The Top Rodeos

Rodeos are more popular than ever. Clowns and riders ply their craft in shows throughout the West, including western Canada:

- **Cheyenne Frontier Days** Held in Cheyenne, Wyoming, in late July, this event is known as the "daddy of 'em all." Begun in 1897, it is one of the most eagerly anticipated events of the rodeo season.

- **Calgary Stampede** This is Canada's biggest rodeo event. Held in July in Calgary, Alberta, the Stampede got its start in 1912. Since 2000, it has been attracting more than 1.2 million rodeo fans a year.

- **Rodeo Houston** This rodeo is held every March in Houston, Texas, in conjunction with the Houston Livestock show. In recent years, it has attracted nearly 2 million attendees over the course of the twenty-day event.

- **La Fiesta De Los Vaqueros** With a name that means "Party of the Cowboys," this weeklong celebration of the Wild West takes place in Tucson, Arizona, in February.

- **Prescott Frontier Days** Held in Prescott, Arizona, this event runs for a week around the Fourth of July. It is billed as the World's Oldest Rodeo in honor of the original Fourth of July event held there in 1864.

- **Southwest Exposition Livestock Show and Rodeo** This three-week event is held in Fort Worth, Texas, beginning in January. It has been running since 1904.

- **Wrangler National Finals Rodeo** The Wrangler National Finals Rodeo is held in Las Vegas, Nevada, in December. It is considered the Super Bowl of rodeo, attracting the top fifteen cowboys and cowgirls in the United States competing for world champion titles.

Rodeo Clowns

When not trying to distract bulls, a rodeo clown's job is to make the audience laugh. A rodeo clown rides a chicken cart in this picture. The "legs" hanging from the end of the cart are false. The clown's real legs are inside the cart, moving it along.

fireworks, clown cars ...This part requires charisma, creativity, comic timing, and boundless energy."

But the clown's real work is to protect the cowboy, a job that requires nerves of steel, the reflexes of a trained athlete, and selfless devotion to the well-being of others.

In her book *Rodeo: An Anthropologist Looks at the Wild and the Tame*, author Elizabeth Atwood Lawrence states, "A bull-fighting clown is a top athlete, and must be fearless as well as agile to successfully perform the function of protecting the contestant."

Scooter Culbertson is a Texas-based barrelman who has been with rodeos since he was sixteen years old and has suffered twenty-four broken bones, three concussions, a dislocated jaw, and other injuries in the course of his career. He agrees that protecting the cowboy is the most important part of his job. "It's a great feeling when the crowd applauds and appreciates your efforts," he told Salary.com. "But the greatest is when the cowboys come to you and let you know how much they appreciate you being there for them night after night."

According to a study by the American Medical Equestrian Association covering the period of 1981 to 1990, rodeo clowns and bullfighters "were, as could be expected, the most frequently injured non-contestants," accounting for almost 83 percent of rodeo-related injuries. "The most injured sites were constant during the ten-year-period with the spine, knee, and shoulder ranking one, two, and three ... however concussion remained the most frequent major injury."

Dwayne Hargo *(left)*, Quail Dobbs *(center)*, and Rick Chatman rush to the aid of a cowboy on the ground. This photo was taken at the 1997 Frontier Days rodeo in Cheyenne, Wyoming. Each rider spends only a few minutes near a bull in a competition. The clowns, however, must face them all day.

Like any other athlete, today's rodeo clowns have their own specialized equipment. While in the old days a clown wore little more for protection than his baggy dungarees, bandanna, and hat, the modern clown is protected by state-of-the-art chest, back, and groin padding as well as knee and shin pads. Instead of cowboy boots, they now wear athletic shoes with cleats for better maneuverability in the arena. They also wear specially designed breakaway pants over colorful tights, in case their clothing gets hooked by a bull's horns.

Jasbo Fulkerson's barrel has also undergone some changes since its introduction in the 1930s. The "clown lounge," as some call it, is now made of heavy-gauge steel and weighs about 175 pounds (79 kilograms). Handholds are welded onto the inside of the barrel, which is lined with industrial foam rubber. In his interview on

Using his barrel to get close enough to the bull, Todd Bowman does a hat trick during a bullfighting competition. at a North Dakota rodeo in 1995. Bullfighting contests allow rodeo clowns to show off all their daredevil skills. They can do tricks and stunts that they can't always do when they're busy saving lives.

Salary.com, Scooter Culbertson makes it clear that while the barrel protects the barrelman, it's by no means invincible. "I spend anywhere from fifteen minutes to an hour after every show pounding out the dents with a five-pound [2.3 kg] mallet," he said.

In 1953, barrelman Jimmy Schumacher of Phoenix, Arizona, introduced the Walking Barrel, which he patented in 1954. This is a barrel open at both ends, allowing the performer to pick it up and maneuver around the arena. To the same end, Billy Keen invented the Bull Machine, a barrel outfitted with wheels and cranks that the barrelman can turn to make the barrel move.

Regardless of the equipment they wear or the props they use, the rodeo clown really relies on nothing so much as his skill and courage.

TODAY'S CLOWNS

While there are competitions for rodeo clowns, they are in fact judged every time they enter the arena. They are judged on their ability to make audiences laugh and, in the case of bullfighters and barrelmen, on how well they safeguard the riders.

Being a rodeo clown is dangerous, yet it is a job many find themselves unable to resist. Like Rob Smets, Nick Jensen of Idaho got his start as a bull rider in high school. At the age of sixteen, Jensen was the Intermountain Professional Rodeo Association's Rookie of the Year, earning a full scholarship to the College of Southern Idaho, a leading rodeo college. In 1997, he won the Rocky Mountain Region Bullriding Championship and secured a spot in the College National Finals Rodeo. Throughout his career, Jensen had recognized the importance of the bullfighter. Out of curiosity, he tried his hand at it and discovered that this was the challenge he'd been seeking.

Arkansas clown James "Buster" Berry found his way to clowning by way of professional stock car racing, exchanging his car for a barrel. As of 2005, Buster was still working the smaller rodeo circuits in the South and the West with his "Sheriff of Clown County" car act, but he dreams of becoming a clown in the PRCA.

Bert Davis, "The Coppertown Clown," started bullfighting and clowning at sixteen and gained fame as the leading animal trainer for rodeo acts. In 1974, the sixteen-year-old Bert was the youngest PRCA rodeo clown in America. In 2003, he was nominated for the PRCA Comedy Act of the Year.

Rodeo clown Bronc Hotsenpiller moves into position as the rider prepares to dismount. The event was part of the 1995 Missouri High School Rodeo. Many stars of the rodeo got their start during high school. Students can compete in many of the same events that are featured in professional rodeos. A new generation of rodeo clowns will come from these young contestants.

Steve Tomac of St. Anthony, North Dakota, had to give up being a full-time clown and barrelman when he joined Congress. He was elected to the North Dakota State Senate in 1991 after serving two terms in the House of Representatives. A PRCA member since 1982, Tomac saw some similarities between his two jobs. "The objective in both is to keep ahead of the bull," he said in a 1991 interview for *ProRodeo Sports News*. "And the timing I use as a clown has helped me in politics, because timing is everything." While in the Senate, Tomac continued to work thirty to fifty rodeos a year.

INTERVIEW WITH CLINT "WOMBLE" DOLAN

In October 2004, Jenaya Murray, the coordinator of the Bullriding Australia Supporters Club, interviewed Clint Dolan. Dolan, who goes by the name of Womble, refers to himself as a professional protection athlete rather than a rodeo clown.

Q: Where did you grow up?

A: I grew up in a small town of 150 people called Croydon which is in the gulf of Queensland. I lived there until I went off to boarding school at Abergowrie College, Ingham.

Q: Bullfighting is a very dangerous sport, and I'm sure one thing on people's minds is why did you decide to do this sport?

A: I rode bulls and did a lot of contract bull catching so I was working a lot with bulls, then one day I got the opportunity to clown a bull and went on from there. It's something I enjoy. I was no good at riding them, but this is something I'm good at.

Q: How long have been in this sport?

A: I started in 1987 and had four years off in 1999 till 2003, so about thirteen years.

Rodeo is an international sport. Although most rodeos are held in North America, they are also popular in countries such as Australia and New Zealand. Australian rodeos are regulated by the Australian Professional Rodeo Association (APRA), which was founded in 1944. In this photo, a bull collides with a rodeo clown at an Australian rodeo in 1994.

Q: I understand you play a very important part in the Bullriding arena. What exactly does a professional protection athlete do?

A: Firstly protect the bull riders when they are fallen or hung up, and to help the bulls buck and spin better.

Q: I could imagine the bulls would come after you a lot and that could lead into serious injury. What would be your worst?

A: Well, I've had a few pretty bad ones. I broke my left arm four times, broke my sternum, had both of my ears cut off, busted my knees several times, and had heaps of dislocated fingers.

Q: How do you become a professional protection athlete?

A: I think the best thing is to have some stock knowledge and try to get to bullfighting classes.

Q: What is the difference between you, a professional protection athlete, and an everyday rodeo clown?

A: Well, we are fighting elite bulls day in, day out and we don't have to do comedy, which I choose to do anyway.

Q: What is your training program?

A: Skipping and riding horses.

Q: Who are your greatest influences?

A: Morris Quinn, Rusty Frame, and Gary McPhee.

CONCLUSION

Rodeo clowns may look like they are just fooling around in the arena, but in reality they are highly trained athletes. While it may not seem like a subject that can be studied in school, many high schools do in fact have rodeo teams, most of which are members of the National High School Rodeo Association (NHSRA). The NHSRA held its first National Championship rodeo in Halletsville, Texas, in 1949. Today, the NHSRA has some 12,000 members from thirty-nine states, five Canadian provinces, and Australia. It holds an annual National High School Finals Rodeo at rotating locations around the United States.

The National Intercollegiate Rodeo Association (NIRA) plays the same role for college rodeo programs. The Fifty-sixth Annual College National Finals Rodeo was held in Casper, Wyoming, in 2005. Younger riders can begin learning the ropes through groups belonging to the National Little Britches Rodeo Association (NLBRA) and the National Junior Bull Riders Association (NJBRA).

The College of Southern Idaho offers a two-year athletic program in rodeo that is among the best in the nation. Its team, the Golden Eagles, regularly competes against four-year schools. In the more than a quarter of a century that Shawn Davis, a three-time world champion saddle bronc rider, has headed the program, it has won twenty-four regional championships, twenty-three top ten national finishes, and three National Intercollegiate Rodeo championships.

The Sankey Rodeo Schools of Branson, Missouri, offer seminars and classes in clowning and bullfighting across the United States. The classes are all taught by championship clowns, including Cory Wall, Bennie Patrick, and Kevin Higley.

One thing that can't be taught at any school is the heartfelt desire to bring laughter and joy to an audience. Clowns, bullfighters, and barrelmen are the heart of the rodeo, bringing laughter to all, but for their part in safeguarding the men and women engaged in this dangerous sport, they have earned their place as the very soul of rodeo.

List of Champions

These contract personnel have been inducted into the ProRodeo Hall of Fame and Museum of the American Cowboy. Contract personnel include rodeo clowns, bullfighters, barrelmen, announcers, and other men and women who help make rodeos happen.

NAME	YEAR INDUCTED
June Ivory	2004
Bob Tallman	2004
Cecil Cornish	2003
Nancy Sheppard	2003
Quail Dobbs	2002
Edith Happy Connelly	2002
Jay Sisler	2002
Jerry Olson	2001
Jo Decker	2001
Tom Hadley	2001
George Doak and Junior Meek	2000
Hadley Barrett	1999
Andy Womack	1998
Gene and Bobby Clark	1997
Pete Logan	1996
Ellen Backstrom	1995
Chuck Henson	1995
Montie Montana	1994
Glenn Randall	1993
Mel Lambert	1990
Wilbur Plaugher	1990
Chuck Parkison	1989

List of Champions

NAME	YEAR INDUCTED
Jimmy Schumacher	1979
Dudley J. Gaudin	1979
George Mills	1979
Homer Holcomb	1979
Jasbo Fulkerson	1979
Wick Peth	1979

Glossary

bareback bronc A bronc whose rider isn't using a saddle but is hanging on courtesy of a strap around the horse's rib cage.

barrelman A rodeo clown who hides in a barrel until he is needed to distract a dangerous bull from injuring a thrown rider.

Brahman bull A breed of bull famous for its ferocity and speed in the arena.

bronc An unbroken, or wild, mustang (horse).

bullfighter In the rodeo, a clown who specializes in distracting the bull long enough to allow a downed rider to get to safety.

bull riding The rodeo event in which a bull is ridden with one hand by a cowboy, who cannot touch anything with his free hand in the eight seconds before the buzzer.

chute The gate from behind which the rodeo animals are released.

rodear A Spanish word meaning "to encircle, or surround," from which comes the word "rodeo."

steer A castrated bull.

stock The animals, or livestock, such as horses, steers, and Brahman bulls, used in the rodeo.

trick ride An acrobatic performance on horseback involving great skill, poise, and style.

vaquero Spanish for "cow man," from which comes the English word "cowboy."

For More Information

National High School Rodeo Association
12001 Tejon Street, Suite 128
Denver, CO 80234
(800) 466-4772
Web site: http://www.nhsra.org

National Intercollegiate Rodeo Association
2316 Eastgate North, #160
Walla Walla, WA 99362
(509) 529-4402
Web site: http://www.collegerodeo.com

National Little Britches Rodeo Association
1045 West Rio Grande
Colorado Springs, CO 80906
(800) 763-3694
Web site: http://www.nlbra.org

Professional Rodeo Cowboys Association
101 Pro Rodeo Drive
Colorado Springs, CO 80919-2301
(719) 593-8840
Web site: http://www.prorodeo.org

Professional Women's Rodeo Association
1235 Lake Plaza Drive, Suite 127
Colorado Springs, CO 80906
(719) 576-1386
Web site: http://www.wpra.com

Rodeo Clowns

ProRodeo Hall of Fame and Museum of the American Cowboy
101 ProRodeo Drive
Colorado Springs, CO 80919
(719) 528-4761
Web site: http://www.prorodeo.org/hof

Sankey Rodeo Schools
3943 Sycamore Church Road
Branson, MO 65616
(417) 334-2513
Web site: http://www.sankeyrodeo.com

WEB SITES

Due to the changing nature of Internet links, the Rosen Publishing Group, Inc., has developed an online list of Web sites related to the subject of this book. This site is updated regularly. Please use this link to access the list:

http://www.rosenlinks.com/woro/rocl

For Further Reading

Campion, Lynn. *Rodeo: Behind the Scenes at America's Most Exciting Sport.* Chester, CT: The Lyons Press, 2002.

Crum, Robert. *Let's Rodeo!: Young Buckaroos and the World's Wildest Sport.* New York, NY: Simon & Schuster Children's Publishing, 1996.

Greenberg, Keith Elliot. *Rodeo Clown: Laughs and Danger in the Ring* (Risky Business). Bellevue, WA: Blackbirch Press, 1995.

Hartnagle-Taylor, Jeanne Joy. *Greasepaint Matadors: The Unsung Heroes of Rodeo.* Loveland, CO: Alpine Publications, Inc., 1992.

Mahoney, Sylvia Gann. *College Rodeo: From Show to Sport* (Centennial Series of the Association of Former Students, Texas A&M University). College Station, TX: Texas A&M University Press, 2004.

McLeese, Tex. *Rodeo Barrel Racing* (Rodeo Discovery Library). Vero Beach, FL: Rourke Publishing, 2000.

Woerner, Gail Hughbanks. *Fearless Funnymen: The History of the Rodeo Clown.* Austin, TX: Eakin Press, 1993.

Bibliography

Clancy, Foghorn. *My Fifty Years in the Rodeo*. San Antonio, TX: The Naylor Co., 1948.

Haber, Jonathan. "Vaqueros: The First Cowboys of the Open Range." *National Geographic News*. November 15, 2003. Retrieved December 23, 2004 (http://news.nationalgeographic.com/news/2003/08/0814_030815_cowboys.html).

Hanesworth, Robert D. *Daddy of 'Em All: The Story of Cheyenne Frontier Days*. Cheyenne, WY: Flintrock Publishing, 1967.

Ingram, Wayne, and Jane Pattie. *Jasbo*. San Antonio, TX: The Naylor Co., 1959.

Lamb, Gene. *Rodeo: Back of the Chutes*. Denver, CO: Multi-List, Inc., 1986.

Lawrence, Elizabeth Atwood. *Rodeo: An Anthropologist Looks at the Wild and the Tame*. Chicago, IL: University of Chicago Press, 1982.

Porter, Willard H. "A Clown from Another Time." *Western Horseman*, May 1984.

Porter, Willard H. "It's Time to Send in the Clowns." *Daily Oklahoman*, August 7, 1987.

Savitt, Sam. *Rodeo—Cowboys, Bulls and Broncos*. New York, NY: Doubleday, 1963.

Sheppard, Lauren. "Dream Job: Rodeo Clown." Retrieved December 23, 2004 (http://www.salary.com/careers/layouthtmls/crel_display_Cat10_Ser185_Par284.html).

Woerner, Gail Hughbanks. *Fearless Funnymen: The History of the Rodeo Clown*. Austin, TX: Eakin Press, 1993.

Index

ABOUT THE AUTHOR

Paul Kupperberg is a writer and an editor for DC Comics. He has worked on more than 700 comic books, stories, articles, and books, as well as several years worth of the *Superman* and *Tom and Jerry* newspaper comic strips. Paul lives in Connecticut with his wife, Robin, and son, Max.

PHOTO CREDITS

Cover, pp. 1, 22, 25, 26, 31, 32, 34 AP/Wide World Photo; p. 4–5 © Omni Photo Communications Inc./Index Stock Imagery, Inc.; p. 7 Library of Congress Prints and Photographs Division; p. 8 © The Granger Collection, New York. p. 9 Cheyenne Frontier Days, 1908, Box 18/Folder 18 National Cowboy & Western Heritage Museum, Oklahoma City, OK; p. 11 © Farrell Grehan/Corbis; pp. 14, 20 photos courtesy of Phillip L. Sublett; p. 16 photo courtesy of Old West Magazine; p. 17 © Bettmann/Corbis; p. 18 Tad Lucas studio portrait, 1935 ca., photographed by Ralph R. Doubleday, Ralph R. Doubleday Collection, #79.026.1938 National Cowboy & Western Heritage Museum, Oklahoma City, OK; p. 19 Foghorn Clancy standing with rope, 1945 ca., photographed by Ralph R. Doubleday, Ralph R. Doubleday Collection, #79.026.2067 National Cowboy & Western Heritage Museum, Oklahoma City, OK; p. 21 Courtesy of The Ponca City News; p. 28 © National Geographic/Getty Images; p. 30 © Gunter Marx Photography/Corbis; p. 36 Stuart Milligan/Allsport.

Designer: Les Kanturek